Well-Schooled Fish and FEATHERED BANDITS

The Wondrous Ways Animals Learn from Animals

Peter Christie

annick press

toronto + new york + vancouver

Text © 2006 Peter Christie
Illustrations © 2006 Warren Clark
Annick Press Ltd.

We acknowledge the support of the Canada Council for the Arts, the Ontario Arts Council, the Government of Canada through the Book Publishing Industry Development Program (BPIDP), and the Ontario Book Publishing Tax Credit (OBPTC) for our publishing activities.

Edited by Elizabeth McLean
Copy-edited by Lori Burwash
Cover and interior design by Warren Clark

Cataloguing in Publication

Christie, Peter, 1962–
Well-schooled fish and feathered bandits: the wondrous ways animals learn from animals /
by Peter Christie.

Includes index. ISBN-13: 978-1-55451-046-7 (bound) ISBN-10: 1-55451-046-5 (bound)
ISBN-13: 978-1-55451-045-0 (pbk.) ISBN-10: 1-55451-045-7 (pbk.)

1. Learning in animals—Juvenile literature. I. Title.
QL785.C47 2006   j591.5'14   C2006-900829-9

591.5,4
CHR
C.

Printed and bound in China

Published in the U.S.A. by
Annick Press (U.S.) Ltd.

Distributed in Canada by
Firefly Books Ltd.
66 Leek Crescent
Richmond Hill, ON
L4B 1H1

Distributed in the U.S.A. by
Firefly Books (U.S.) Inc.
P.O. Box 1338
Ellicott Station
Buffalo, NY 14205

Visit our website at www.annickpress.com

Photo credits
Front cover, 6: © First Light/Roger Wilmhurst/Foto Natura; **5:** © iStockphoto.com/John Christian; **8, 22:** © Heather Angel/Natural Visions; **9:** © C. Andrew Henley/Natural Visions; **11:** © First Light/Fred Bavendam; **12, 38:** © First Light/Flip Nicklin; **13:** © iStockphoto.com/Steve Irwin; **14:** © iStockphoto.com/Mike Ludkowski; **15:** © First Light/Mike Powles; **16:** © First Light/Shin Yoshino; **17:** © iStockphoto.com/Graeme Purdy; **18, 21:** © Jakob Dulisse; **19:** © iStockphoto.com/Amanda Rohde; **23:** © iStockphoto.com/Sue McDonald; **24:** © First Light/Oxford Scientific Film; **25:** © James R. Page; **27:** © First Light/Clive Bromhall; **28:** © Michael Heithaus; **29:** © First Light/Kelvin Aitken; **31:** © iStockphoto.com/Sheri Bigelow; **33:** © iStockphoto.com/Peter Llewellyn; **34:** First Light/Thomas Kitchin & Victoria Hurst; **35:** © First Light/Frans Lanting; **36:** © iStockphoto.com/Sean Morris; **37:** © First Light/Premium Stock; **40:** © iStockphoto.com/Marco Kopp; **41:** © First Light/Tanya Constantine

For Hannah and Laura, of course.

Introduction

COIN CRIME AND CREAM THIEVES

A car wash coin machine in Fredericksburg, Virginia, was losing hundreds of dollars in quarters each week. To catch the thief, the puzzled owner installed a hidden camera. The photos showed not one bandit, but many— and they weren't dishonest employees. They were birds! And they were working as a gang.

Starlings are fond of shiny things, and these mottled black European starlings had discovered a glittery stash in the coin machine.

European starlings are smart birds— several ganged up to steal money from a coin machine.

The starlings found that they could climb into the machine through the coin slot. Once inside, they could peck free quarters by the beakful. One bird would dislodge the quarters while others waited to make off with the loot. It was organized crime. The trick was likely discovered by one bird, but the starlings soon learned from one another.

Humans don't usually think of animals learning from one another. We tend to think of them doing what they do and liking what they like because it's in their nature. We call it instinct. It's something all animals are born with.

Instinct *is* important, and so is individual experience. But researchers are beginning to discover just how many animals also learn from one another through social contact. This is known as social learning.

Scientists first noticed how valuable social learning can be for animals

One tasty breakfast for this bird will leave one unhappy milk customer.

about 50 years ago. That's when research revealed that several bird species in Britain were learning from one another how to raid milk bottles delivered to people's doorsteps. The birds were pecking through the foil caps to drink the cream. The trick, which annoyed morning tea drinkers, spread across the country and into Europe.

Around the same time, a group of macaque monkeys in Japan was observed learning to wash sweet potatoes in water to remove sand. A local innkeeper scattered the potatoes on the beach so she and her guests could watch the monkeys eat. One monkey, named Imo, had discovered the art of washing her food, and the rest had copied her behavior.

Individual learning can lead to fatal mistakes. Sometimes it's safer for an animal to copy another.

Learning from parents or others in a group is essential for people—and for animals too. Discovering how to eat or where to find food can mean the difference between starvation and survival.

Scientists are realizing that many other life-and-death lessons are passed along from animal to animal, such as how to avoid predators or how to get along in a group. Social learning about courtship can affect whether or not an animal mates to pass its genes to a new generation. And it helps creatures understand their changing world more quickly without being killed or injured by trial-and-error learning.

No more sandy suppers! Japanese macaque monkeys copied one monkey's idea to wash her sweet potatoes.

Chapter One

THE RATTY GOURMET

For a rat, it's a good thing when a place gets down in the dumps. After the Second World War, Berlin, Germany, was a mess, with whole sections of the city in ruins from bombing. The rats were having a heyday.

Rats learn from other rats where to find good grub and how to avoid poisoned food.

Fritz Steiniger wanted to change that. No run-of-the-mill rat catcher, Steiniger was a scientist, an educated rat buster. He made sure that the poisoned bait he set out in rat-infested areas never ran low. A steady supply, he thought, would guarantee that every rat in the area would eventually eat it and die.

Wrong. His plan failed, and the rats thrived.

At first, a lot of rats died. But some only tasted the poison. Although these rats became ill, they survived and never touched the bait again. Even more amazing was the fact that the young of these survivor rats didn't eat the poisoned bait either. They wouldn't even try it.

Scientists now know that young rats, such as those born to survivors of Steiniger's poison, rely on social learning to understand much about what and what not to eat. While nursing, they learn about foods their mother eats from flavors in her milk. Sometimes they learn by watching adults eat or by following adult-made scent trails to meals. They even learn to prefer food that's near the feces and urine of other rats! It means that rats were happily and safely feeding there earlier.

When food tastes bad, rats grimace like a disgusted baby; a "yummy" face means it's good.

But few things excite a ratty appetite as much as good ol' stinky rat breath. Rats sniff the breath of other rats to decide what to eat themselves. They may prefer food for a month or longer after smelling it on another rat's breath. Rats will even choose meals they normally wouldn't, such as lunch laced with pepper, if they smell peppery rat breath.

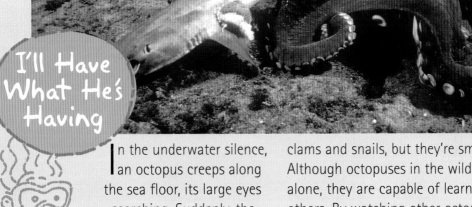

I'll Have What He's Having

In the underwater silence, an octopus creeps along the sea floor, its large eyes searching. Suddenly, the shapeless creature transforms into a sleek, speeding torpedo. Shooting over the sea bottom, it wraps around an unsuspecting reef crab, injects it with paralyzing poison, and begins to feed.

Octopuses may be cousins to simple clams and snails, but they're smart. Although octopuses in the wild live alone, they are capable of learning from others. By watching other octopuses, they can even learn to distinguish easy, tasty prey from prey that hurts to catch, such as an adult spiny lobster.

Learning from the experience of others means keeping your eyes open and using your brain. The discovery of social learning in octopuses suggests that this is an important skill even among such primitive animals.

Many other animals rely on social learning for feeding tips. The killer whales at Marineland in Niagara Falls, Ontario, have apparently learned from one another how to bait and catch gulls. The whales vomit some of their last fishy meal onto the water's surface and wait below to grab gulls that come to feed on it. Likely the brainchild of one clever young whale, four others learned the vomit trick from him.

In Japan, carrion crows use vehicles to crush walnuts for them. The crows set the nuts from nearby trees at intersections and return after the

Staying in schools teaches French grunts where to find the best feeding grounds.

traffic has passed. The trick appears to have spread from crow to crow after first being reported near a driving school in Tokyo.

Near the Virgin Islands, French grunts learn in schools. Every dawn and dusk, these coral reef fish travel the same route between their daytime resting places and their feeding grounds. Nothing marks the path. They learn the route only if they school with fish that already know the way.

The minnowlike nine-spined stickleback also finds the best place to eat by following the group—if it doesn't have a better idea from its own experience. If the school is going in one direction and the stickleback knows there's food in another, it will choose to be a fish-school dropout and swim to the sure thing. For sticklebacks, social learning is important, but it sometimes takes a back seat to other ways of learning.

Japan's carrion crows discovered an easy way to crack walnuts. They drop them on the road for cars to run over.

Domestic chickens learn from one another too, and sometimes they learn to be cannibals—eating their own kind. It might sound disgusting to us, but hens occasionally enjoy a high-protein meal by attacking and eating the eggs and chicks of other hens. Chicken cannibalism often begins with a small group of birds, but it can spread through a whole flock.

Cannibalism is one of the main causes of death among flocks of egg-laying chickens..

Chapter Two

SNAKE EYES AND MONKEY BUSINESS

Rhesus monkeys have a lot to be nervous about, living in the forests of Asia. Snakes and wild cats prowl the ground. Monkey-eating eagles hunt in the treetops. For a rhesus monkey, knowing who your enemies are could mean the difference between life and death.

Imagine the terror, then, for a rhesus monkey captured from the wild and stuck in a cage with a boa constrictor. This happened in a real experiment. The monkey was frantic and desperate to escape. Rattling the cage, it shrieked its noisy alarm:

Look out! Her face showing her alarm, this rhesus monkey is letting others know there's danger nearby.

Ravens will mob large predators such as this eagle to drive them away. Younger birds can learn to recognize enemies by seeing who gets mobbed.

"Chitter-chut! Chitter-chut!" Its fear of the deadly snake was loud and unmistakable.

Now imagine a group of rhesus monkeys calmly facing a boa constrictor, continuing about their business. The difference? These rhesus monkeys were raised in captivity. When researchers exposed them to the dangerous snake, they had never seen one before and they were not afraid.

Blackbird Bottle Battle

European blackbirds often swoop and badger hawks, owls, and other predators until they fly away. This is called mobbing. Young blackbirds learn to recognize danger by watching flock mates mob enemies.

Researchers tricked young blackbirds into thinking that a harmless friarbird was a threat. Friarbirds eat nectar and insects, not other birds. The young blackbirds watched as older blackbirds in a second cage appeared to mob the friarbird—but were actually mobbing an owl the young birds could not see. Afterward, the young blackbirds mobbed the friarbird, convinced that it was dangerous.

Other blackbirds were shown a plastic bleach bottle. At the same time, researchers played a tape of blackbird alarm calls. After that, the birds declared war on the bottle and mobbed it when they could.

When it comes to knowing enemy from friend, young rhesus monkeys have a lot to learn. And since learning about predators by experience may be deadly, the monkeys learn from one another. Monkeys raised in laboratories are frightened by snakes after they repeatedly see another rhesus monkey react to one with horror—even if they are shown the scene on television.

Social learning is important to rhesus monkeys, but it isn't everything. When scientists played a video of a monkey that appeared to be scared of a flower, the other monkeys weren't convinced. None of them developed a fear of flowers. Instinct seems to help them know what's likely—and what's unlikely—to be dangerous.

Wallabies in Australia learn to fear foxes after seeing others thump their feet or flee at the sight of one.

Monkeys are not the only animals that watch others to learn what to fear. A variety of mammals, birds, and even fish do it too.

Fathead minnows, for instance, are not bothered by the smell of minnow-eating pike—as long as they've never met one before. But if one minnow shows fear of the predator's scent, from then on, the others will dart and hide at the faintest whiff of a pike.

Some animals even learn from one another to avoid being bitten by flies. Deer mice in northern forests learn to hide from black flies and other biting insects. More amazingly, mice that have never been bitten produce a painkiller after seeing other mice react to fly bites. That way, if the mice are bitten, it will hurt less.

Fly bites hurt, but deer mice learn from one another how to hide from the pests.

Chapter three

THE HOTTEST BIRD IN THE BARN

It's April and in the quail coop of a country barn, a bird version of romance is in the air. Japanese quail are raised by farmers who sell their eggs and meat. But on this spring day, several female Japanese quail are looking to choose a mate. One pauses when she sees a male across the coop.

The bird—let's call her Juliet—is smitten: Romeo is the quail of her dreams. She quickly waddles toward him.

If those females like him, he must be a good catch... Female Japanese quail prefer males that attract other females.

But wait. Juliet glances to the left and sees a male she hadn't noticed before. She stops and stares.

The second male is surrounded by other females, all appearing to want his attention. To Juliet, a male that seems to be the choice of other females is impossible to ignore. She turns. Romeo is history.

This scene is imaginary, but it's based on actual laboratory experiments with quail. Many female animals are thought to be acting on instinct when they choose a mate. They are programmed by nature to pick the most attractive or the strongest males in order to produce the best possible youngsters. Making a mistake about a mate could result in having young with weak genes, who may not survive to become adults or may be too weak and unattractive to mate and raise young of their own.

For quail, social learning about mates may seem riskier than following their instincts, but it allows a shortcut in their decision making. As long as other female quail are good judges of quality males, a quail has a better chance of picking a worthy mate by copying them. And

Quail will even copy the choices of females they see on television.

she's spared the time and energy of figuring this out for herself.

In brown-headed cowbird courtship, social learning works for both males and females. The males learn their songs from other males in their flock, and their burbling songs are performed differently depending on where they live.

Male brown-headed cowbirds want to impress their audience. They repeat songs that get the best response from females.

Good Golly, Miss Molly

Sometimes one species of animal can learn from another. In one case, this type of learning helps to prevent the extinction of one kind of fish altogether.

With no males of their own kind, female Amazon mollies must mate with males of a related fish, the sailfin molly, to produce eggs. But male sailfin mollies can't fertilize Amazon molly eggs, so none of the youngsters belong to them. These mixed matings wouldn't make sense for male sailfins if it weren't for social learning. Sailfin molly females copy the mate choices of other female sailfins—and also copy Amazon mollies. A male sailfin that mates with an Amazon molly becomes more attractive to females of his own species.

A female cowbird prefers males who sing tunes that are similar to the ones she heard when she was young. The songs of males from a different place just aren't as attractive. If males see that a female approves (by flapping her wings, for example), they will sing that song more often. They learn from her response to change their musical program.

Like Japanese quail, female guppies prefer males that appear to be attracting

Female guppies will prefer colorful males unless they've seen other females choose dull ones.

A male three-spined stickleback with eggs in his nest is more attractive to a female.

young guppies are most likely to follow the example of an older guppy.

other females. If a female guppy sees other females choose a dull-colored male over a more colorful one, she will prefer that male—and other dull males in general—from then on.

Another female fish, the three-spined stickleback, prefers males with eggs already in their nests. Among sticklebacks, the males build nests and guard the eggs. Female sticklebacks cruising for a mate like to survey a male's domestic setup first. If a male has eggs in his nest, another female must have chosen him. If another female picked him, he must be a good catch.

Chapter Four

THE INSPECTOR GADGET OF CROWS

Deep in a South Seas island forest, a hoarse voice cries in the wilderness: "Waaw, waaw!" The call belongs to a crow in a palmlike tree called a screw pine.

The crow bites and pulls at the tree's long, stiff leaves. It flies off, carrying a long hooked cutting from the leaf in its bill, and lands in a nearby tree. Carefully, the crow pokes the strip beneath the tree's bark. It dislodges a juicy grub and quickly gobbles it down.

Learning to use a human invention, such as a water fountain, is good enough for some clever crows. But others in the South Seas have invented tools of their own.

Welcome to New Caledonia in the South Pacific, east of Australia. Although the New Caledonian crows look like a huskier version of our common crow, there's an important difference: the crows here are remarkable toolmakers.

Tools may seem like a very human invention, but they are also used by a number of birds, mammals, and other animals (even some ants). The New Caledonian crows, however, are unusual because they not only use leaf cuttings as tools but also modify the cuttings. They carefully add notches to make the tool work better, and may even pass tool-design improvements to other crows.

Until the New Caledonian crows were studied, many people assumed that only humans were capable of improving tools and passing on that know-how. Our ability to do this has steadily improved our technology. For the crows, it's an important achievement that appears to make their hunting easier.

New Caledonian crows are "right-handed." Like humans, they show a right-side bias when using tools.

Female bottlenose dolphins in Shark Bay, Australia, also learn a tool trick from one another. Their trick appears to be something daughters learn from their mothers. The habit likely began with a single "inventor mom" and then spread by social learning.

The dolphins scoop up marine sponges that they wear on their snout (called a rostrum) while they root around in the seabed. The sponge may help prevent cuts or scratches, like a

The Ant Fishers of Gombe

Chimpanzees in the wild use tools, such as rocks, to crack nuts. They also use stick rods to "fish" ants or termites out of holes. Pulling the insects off the sticks with their lips, the chimps enjoy a crunchy lunch.

At Tanzania's Gombe National Park in East Africa, chimps fish with long sticks. In West Africa, chimps use shorter ones. If the behavior were instinctive or learned by individuals, the sticks used by the two groups would likely be similar. The different lengths suggest that chimps are learning the skill from others in their group, and copying the stick length as well.

protective glove. Most male dolphins and even other females in the same area have yet to catch on to the idea.

The ability to use tools doesn't always mean social learning is at work, however. Tool use can also be instinctive. For instance, the woodpecker finches of the Galápagos Islands are famous for using twigs and cactus spines to prod insects out of tree bark. In this species, though, tool use is a skill that the birds appear to come by instinctively. They use sticks and spines even if they've never seen another finch demonstrate the trick.

Some bottlenose dolphins in Australia wear sponges to protect their snouts when they probe the sea floor for food.

Chapter Five

A COLOSSAL CHANGE IN TUNE

Far out in the Pacific Ocean, the vast blue-black back of a whale breaks the surface. It arches, sliding deeper, and with a final wave of enormous flukes in the air, it disappears under the water. A humpback is on the move.

In the late 1990s, singing humpback whales in the Pacific Ocean experienced a musical revolution.

Humpback whales migrate between summer feeding grounds in polar oceans and winter breeding areas in faraway tropical waters. As they swim, the graceful giants, each as heavy as six adult male Asian elephants, sing like no other animal on Earth.

"Eeeeeeeiiiooooaarrr." The whales' slow, mournful music of whistles, squeals, grunts, and sighs is hauntingly beautiful. Each song can last up to 20 minutes and be heard across the ocean. This may help explain why whales living throughout the same ocean sing a similar tune.

Humpbacks seem to learn their songs through social learning. Small changes to these tunes are introduced every year, and they appear to spread from whale to whale throughout an ocean. Even so, the humpback songs in different oceans— the Pacific, Atlantic, and Indian—are distinct from one another.

In 1996, scientists using underwater microphones to record whale songs in the Pacific Ocean off Australia's east coast discovered something startling: 2 of the 82 humpbacks they heard were singing a new and totally different tune. By the next year, several

Humpback whale music may be for serenading females or for warning away rival males.

Parrot "Chat Clubs"

Parrots are great talkers. Raised as pets, yellow-naped Amazon parrots are famous for imitating human speech (even if they don't know what they're saying). In the wilds of South and Central America, these bright green parrots have another use for their remarkable learning skills: membership in parrot "chat clubs."

In large neighboring areas, hundreds of parrots form groups. They know which parrots belong to their group because each group has a distinctive way of calling. The interesting thing about these "chat clubs" is that they are not exclusive. Parrots from one club can easily join another, and they often do. The only requirement is that new members learn the dialect of their new group. For parrots, it pays to be a lifelong learner.

Parrots of all kinds call and squawk to one another. Some species are just chattier than others.

other Pacific Ocean whales were singing the new song, and in 1998, every whale they recorded sang only that tune. The old song had been abandoned.

The researchers had witnessed a kind of whale-sized pop music revolution. The new tune was similar to the song sung by Indian Ocean whales, on the other side of Australia. A small number of singers must have crossed over, and the new song caught on with Pacific Ocean whales.

Since then, the Pacific song and the Indian Ocean song have both been changing, bit by bit, year by year. Once again, they are becoming distinct from each other.

Small, local differences in songs might result when one bird's song-learning mistakes are copied and shared.

Catchy tunes are common in the world of singing birds. Most songbirds learn their often elaborate melodies by listening to other songbirds. No one really knows why these birds learn (singing frogs, for instance, are born with songs already in their heads). But songbird learning is one of the best-known examples of social learning in animals.

Like many other songbirds, white-crowned sparrows sing slightly different songs (called dialects) depending on where they live. They're like people from different places who talk with different accents.

While some birds learn music directly from their fathers, these sparrows learn after they have moved away and settled into a new neighborhood. There, they copy the dialect sung by

White-crowned sparrows wait until they're settled into a neighborhood to learn the songs their new neighbors sing.

others in the area. For sparrows, this appears to be an important part of fitting in.

Killer whales have dialects too. They communicate with one another using whistles and clicks that may be passed from whale to whale. But many calls are shared only within closely related killer whale groups (called pods) and not with other killer whales swimming in the area.

Killer whales in the same pod talk to each other with clicks and whistles.

Chapter Six

THE HAIRY DOLL-MAKER

As the sun disappears from a gloomy, mosquito-infested swamp on Borneo, an orangutan settles comfortably into its treetop nest. There, high above the damp, the great red-haired ape's carefully constructed bed is downright cozy. She gazes through the leaves at the twilight. Then, before she drifts off to sleep, she hugs her handmade doll to her chest.

Making drinking cups from leaves is one of many orangutan habits that seem surprisingly like human behavior.

Huh? Her doll?

It's true. Life in the trees on the islands of Borneo and Sumatra, home to the last of the orangutans, includes many habits that are surprisingly like human behaviors. Some orangutans (from the Malay phrase meaning "forest person") cradle a bundle of leaves like a doll. Some also use carefully shaped sticks as tools, and leaves as napkins or gloves. They even make drinking cups or water sponges from foliage, build roofs for their nests, and cut vines for swinging, Tarzan-style, through the trees.

The tradition of "dolls" among some of Borneo's orangutans is amazing. Also interesting is the fact that orangutans in several other Borneo populations and in nearby Sumatra don't make dolls at all. Researchers studying the apes in six isolated areas on the islands reported doll cuddling in only two of these locations.

Seals and sea lions are a favorite food of killer whales.

A Whale of a Teacher

On the sunny shore of the Crozet Islands in the South Indian Ocean, elephant seals are basking quietly. Suddenly a dark shape appears in the sea. Whoosh! A killer whale bursts from the water and hits the beach. With half her body ashore, the whale grabs a seal pup in her jaws, then wriggles back into the water.

Snatching a seal from land is amazing—and risky. A whale could easily strand itself. What's even more amazing is the possibility that whales may teach this dangerous stunt to their young. Young killer whales have been seen carefully watching nearby while their mothers apparently demonstrate shoreline seal snatching.

A lot of animals learn by watching others, but teachers do things for no other reason than to pass on lessons. Although many people believe that only humans can teach, some biologists are convinced that these whales actively teach this trick to their young.

A tradition shared among members of only one group suggests that the behavior shows up only where animals learn it from one another. And this type of learning is not just about dolls. Many orangutan behaviors are practiced in some places but not in others.

In Africa, chimpanzees dance when it rains. No one knows why. In Tanzania, in southeast Africa, the rain dance is a wild boogie-woogie compared to the chimp rain dance

Sperm whales learn how to come together as a group to defend themselves.

on the western side of the continent. There, in Ivory Coast, the dance is slow and deliberate and includes aggressive posing, almost like martial arts.

The chimps' dancing, like the orangutans' doll making, is a behavior the apes appear to learn from one another according to local tradition. It is one of many traditions, including using tools, drumming on trees, using leaves as sponges, and making combs, that are performed differently by chimps in different places.

Social learning may also be at work under the sea near Vancouver Island on Canada's west coast. There, some killer whale pods face each other in formal "greeting lines" when they meet, almost like people do at a wedding. Other killer whale groups, even some that live in the same area, don't show this behavior.

Different groups of sperm whales appear to learn from one another how to defend

A high-five handclasp signals it's grooming time for chimps in one Tanzanian forest.

themselves. For instance, some sperm whale groups defend themselves against killer whales by forming a tight rank, facing an attack with their head and jaws. Other groups come together like the spokes of a bicycle wheel, facing one another in the center with their tails pointing out to clobber approaching predators.

The tricks shared and passed down through generations of orangutans, chimps, and perhaps even whales are numerous and seemingly sophisticated. Some argue that this sets them apart from other social learners.

Orangutans were once thought to be less intelligent than chimpanzees. But the red-haired apes also have complex behaviors such as tool making.

Conclusion

LEARNING TO BE DIFFERENT

Social learning can open the door to a whole new way of life for some animals. In Israel's pine forests, colonies of black rats have gone squirrelly. They're acting like squirrels—scampering about, climbing trees, and eating pine seeds. By adapting to the pine forests, they don't have to compete with rats that live in towns and farms and other areas where rats are numerous.

Learning from one another is an important part of being human.

But living in these woods is tough unless you've learned how. Eating pine cone seeds is an art. The trick is to start at the bottom and spiral upward, carefully pulling away each cone scale to uncover the seeds. Rats almost never figure this out on their own. But if their mothers demonstrate the trick, young rats always learn the skill.

In many ways, social learning has changed how these rats get along in the world. It has changed us too. We humans have always depended on our ability to learn from one another— how to speak, how to act, and how to make plans. With every generation, we pass along improved knowledge that helps us to lead longer and very different lives.

When we study animals, we see how important social learning is for them. They sometimes learn and act in ways that appear to be almost human. And as we understand more about this type of learning among animals, we realize that their hand-me-down wisdom may be far more common than we imagined.

young rats learn to strip pine cones by taking partly opened cones from adult rats and finishing the job.

FURTHER READING

Attenborough, David. *The Life of Birds* (video series). London: BBC, 2000. Online resources available at http://www.pbs.org/lifeofbirds/.

Conniff, Richard. *Rats: The Good, The Bad and The Ugly*. New York: Random House, 2002.

Dennard, Deborah, and John F. McGee. *Monkeys (Our Wild World)*. Minnetonka, MN: Northword Press, 2003.

Doris, Ellen. *Ornithology (Real Kids/Real Science Books)*. New York: Thames and Hudson, 1994.

Dudzinski, Kathleen. *Meeting Dolphins*. Washington, DC: National Geographic Children's Books, 2000.

Fink Martin, Patricia A. *Orangutans (True Books)*. Danbury, CT: Children's Press, 2000.

Goodall, Jane. *Chimpanzee Family Book*. New York: North-South Books, 1997.

Goodall, Jane. *My Life with the Chimpanzees*. New York: Aladdin Library, 1996.

Kennett, David. *Killer Whale*. Malvern, Australia: Omnibus Books, 2002.

Lauber, Patricia. *An Octopus Is Amazing (Let's Read-And-Find-Out Science)*. New York: HarperTrophy, 1996.

Milton, Joyce. *Whales: The Gentle Giants*. New York: Random House, 1989.

National Geographic Society. *National Geographic Animal Encyclopedia*. Washington, DC: National Geographic Children's Books, 2000.

Orme, David. *Orangutan (Animals under Threat)*. Portsmouth, NH: Heinemann, 2005.

Platt, Richard, David Burnie, and Jayne Parsons. *Apes (Secret World Series)*. New York: DK Publishing, 2001.

Pringle, Laurence P., and Bob Marstall (illustrator). *Crows! Strange and Wonderful*. Honesdale, PA: Boyds Mills Press, 2002.

Taylor, Barbara. *Apes and Monkeys*. London: Anness Publishing, 2004.

Vogel, Julia. *Dolphins (Our Wild World)*. Minnetonka, MN: Northword Press, 2001.

SELECTED BIBLIOGRAPHY

Bonner, J.T. 1980. *The Evolution of Culture in Animals*. Princeton, NJ: Princeton University Press.

Catchpole, C.K., and P.J.B. Slater. 1995. *Bird Song: Biological Themes and Variations*. Cambridge, UK: Cambridge University Press.

Cloutier, S., R.C. Newberry, K. Honda, and R.J. Alldredge. 2002. Cannibalistic behaviour spread by social learning. *Animal Behaviour* 63: 1153–62.

Dugatkin, L.A. 2000. *The Imitation Factor: Evolution Beyond the Gene*. New York: The Free Press.

Epsmark, Y., T. Amundsen, and G. Rosenquist, eds. 2000. *Animal Signals: Signalling and Signal Design in Animal Communication*. Norway: Tapir Academic Press.

Fiorito, G., and P. Scotto. 1992. Observational learning in *Octopus vulgaris*. *Science* 256: 545–47.

Freeberg, T.M. 2004. Social transmission of courtship behavior and mating preferences in brown-headed cowbirds, *Molothrus ater*. *Learning & Behavior* 32: 122–30.

Galef, B.G., and K.N. Laland. 2005. Social learning in animals: Empirical studies and theoretical models. *BioScience* 55: 489–99.

——— and Catherine Rankin. 1997. Learning under the influence. *Natural History* 106: 47–49.

——— and L. Heiber. 1976. The role of residual olfactory cues in determination of feeding site selection and exploration patterns of domestic rats. *Journal of Comparative and Physiological Psychology* 90: 727–39.

Guinet, C., and J. Bouvier. 1995. Development of intentional stranding hunting techniques in killer whale (*Orcinus orca*) calves at Crozet Archipelago. *Canadian Journal of Zoology* 73: 27–33.

Helfman, G.S., and E.T. Schultz. 1984. Social transmission of behavioural traditions in a coral reef fish. *Animal Behaviour* 32: 379–84.

Heyes, C.M., and B.G. Galef, eds. 1996. *Social Learning in Animals: The Roots of Culture*. San Diego: Academic Press.

Hunt, G.R., and R.D. Gray. 2002. Diversification and cumulative evolution in New Caledonian crow tool manufacture. *Proceedings of the Royal Society London* B 270: 867–74.

Krutzen, M., J. Mann, M.R. Heithaus, R.C. Connor, L. Bejder, and W.B. Sherwin. 2005. Cultural transmission of tool use in bottlenose dolphins. *Proceedings of National Academy of Sciences* 102: 8939–43.

Laland, K.N., and W. Hoppitt. 2003. Do animals have culture? *Evolutionary Anthropology* 12: 150–59.

Mineka, S., M. Davidson, M. Cook, and R. Keir. 1984. Observational conditioning of snake fear in rhesus monkeys. *Journal of Abnormal Psychology* 93: 355–72.

Noad, M.J., D.H. Cato, M.M. Bryden, M-N Jenner, and K.C.S. Jenner. 2000. Cultural revolution in whale songs. *Nature* 408: 537.

Rendell, L., and H. Whitehead. 2001. Culture in whales and dolphins. *Behavioral and Brain Sciences* 24: 309–82.

Schlupp, I., C. Marler, and M.J. Ryan. 1994. Benefit to male sailfin mollies of mating with heterospecific females. *Science* 263: 373–74.

Van Schaik, C.P., M. Ancrenaz, G. Borgen, B. Galdikas, C.D. Knott, I. Singleton, A. Suzuki, S.S. Utami, M. Merrill. 2003. Orangutan cultures and the evolution of material culture. *Science* 299: 102–5.

White, D.J., and B.G. Galef. 2000. "Culture" in quail: Social influences on mate choices of female *Coturnix japonica*. *Animal Behaviour* 59: 975–79.

Whiten, A., J. Goodall, W.C. McGrew, T. Nishida, V. Reynolds, Y. Sugiyama, Y., C.E.G. Tutin, R.W. Wrangham, and C. Boesch. 1999. Cultures in chimpanzees. *Nature*, 399: 682–85.

Wright, T.F., and G.S. Wilkinson. 2001. Population genetic structure and vocal dialects in an amazon parrot. *Proceeding of the Royal Society London B* 268: 609–16.

ACKNOWLEDGMENTS

I would like to thank Professor Kevin Laland at the Centre for Social Learning and Cognitive Evolution, University of St. Andrews, Scotland, for his review of the material in this book and for his comments and suggestions. Dr. Laland, in turn, would like to thank his son Thomas for wondering about his father's work. This book and I also owe a tremendous debt to Elizabeth McLean, Antonia Banyard, Warren Clark, Lori Burwash, and (as always) Priscilla Ferrazzi.